I0284469

Published by:
Powder River Publishing LLC
147 N. Burritt Ave
Buffalo, Wyoming 82834

Copyright © 2021
ISBN: 9781736665985
Printed in the United States of America

No part of this publication may be reproduced, stored, transmitted in any form — electronic, mechanical, digital photocopy, recording, or other without the express written approval of the author.

All rights reserved solely by the author. The author guarantees all are original and do not infringe upon the legal right of any other person or work. The views expressed in this book are not necessarily that of the publisher.

The photography in this book has been gathered from Gene Gagliano, Ryan Collins and Pixabay. It is used with the kind permission of the photographers or owners that are indicated. No photograph may be reproduced without the permission of these owners.

Dedicated to everyone who seeks beauty and truth.

Acknowledgements: Special thanks to Ryan Collins for appreciating my writing and Julie Snyder for her technological assistance. As always thanks to my wife Carol, family and friends for their continued love and support.

Table of Contents

A Song — 1

Behind the Mask — 2

Braids — 3

Bullied — 4

Compassion International — 5

Daddy's Little Princess — 6

Death — 7

Defining Moments — 8

Entering the ER — 9

Everyday Heroes — 10

Fourth Grade — 11

Grandma's Fear — 12

Happy Birthday Gina — 13

Humor — 14

I Believe — 15

Impressions — 16

Letting Go — 17

Like Droplets of Water — 18

Little Children — 19

Little Things — 20

Love Letter — 21

Memories — 22

The Blessing of Wyoming — 23

On a Positive Note — 24

School Teacher — 25

Secret to Longevity — 26

Snippets of a Young Child's Memories — 27

Thank You, Lord — 28

Cleaning Lady — 29

The Gambler — 30

The Old Lady — 31

Twenty-One — 32

Weary Traveler — 33

Wounds — 34

Young Man — 35

Annie — 36

Blue Bird — 37

Bull's Eye — 38

Max — 39

Bridges — 40

Contrast — 41

Dreams in the Wind — 42

Flight — 43

I-25 Cheyenne to Chugwater — 44

Funeral Home — 45

Autumn's Smokey Landscape — 46

Calender of Trees — 47

Winter — 48

Avalanche — 49

Campfire — 50

Dandelion — 51

Darkness — 52

Each Seed — 53

Long Journeys — 54

November Cottonwoods — 55

Phantom Clouds — 56

Silver Lake – 57

Snowflakes — 58

The Birth of Day — 59

Garden Cherubs — 60

The Log — 61

Unnoticed — 62

Water's Power — 63

White Asters — 64

Wrath of the Wind — 65

Wyoming Watershed — 66

April Snow — 67

Wyoming's Palet of Colors — 68

A Song

*Strange, how a song
Can tug at your soul
Lift your spirit
Trigger a smile or
Tap into your well of tears*

*Remind you of
Events and times
People and places
Engraved on your heart
By the pen of life*

*Memories
Instilled by laughter
Heartaches, joy or sorrow
The threads of existence
Woven into your being*

Behind The Mask

behind the mask
the unknown
fear of the what ifs
fear of catching the virus
the sorrow of having lost a loved one
the unhappiness of having to cancel
finishing senior year, graduation, prom
a state sports championship game
postponing a wedding, an anniversary cruise,
a once in a lifetime vacation

behind the mask
someone struggles to survive
a dream for the future may have died
a spouse or friend deals with a loved one's cancer
a surgery or medical procedure is postponed
somebody carries the burden of depression
fear of losing a job, a home, or a business
the building of a new home put on hold
a pregnant mother worries about her unborn child
a family must mourn the loss of a member without a funeral

behind the mask
is so much more than we can see

Braids

My granddaughter's eyes
are dark like mine,
but filled with the promise of youth.
I watch her as she lovingly
braids her mother's hair
with slender fingers.
For a moment
I see the woman in pigtails
become my little girl again.
I'm the proud father
the most important man in her life.
The phone rings and the moment
passes, a call from her husband.

Bullied

Small, thin and weak
An easy target
Third to eighth grade
Like prey for a carnivore

So much hurt
Memories that
Still haunt me
Into my old age

Too afraid
To dunk my head
Under the water
To pick up the ring

Boys taunting me
Down the hallway
From over the edges
Of a lavatory stall

Always last to be called
To play on a team
The major target
For a game of Dodge Ball

Headed to school
The constant teasing
From swearing boys
On the back of the bus

The coach that allowed
The teasing while
I stood in the shallow
End of the pool

The pushing and shoving
The name calling
The insults and object
Of hurtful jokes

Kids grabbing my lunch
And playing catch
Poking and bumping
Knocking me on the head

Compassion International

Children are the flowers
In a parent's garden of love.

A child is like a flowering plant
Needs nurturing to make it grow and bloom.
Needs somebody to love and care for it
Provide food and water, warmth and light,
And protect it from the storm.

Like a flower bud in a cottage garden
Its potential is unknown,
Until it burst forth into bloom.
Like a blossom, each child is unique,
With its own color, shape and size,
But without the right conditions
Cannot obtain its full potential.

Compassion International is like the gardener
Who helps provide the necessary conditions
When parents can't meet their needs
For child growth and development.
Every child is a part of the human family
Regardless of race, color or creed.

Let us be part of the parent's garden of love
And with kindness and caring
Help Compassion International
Make each child become
All they can be.

Daddy's Little Princess

Imagine her
as a child
bright eyed, long hair
full of life
singing and dancing
energetic, imaginative
eager to learn
mama's helper
daddy's little princess

She sits quietly
in the nursing home
slumped in her wheelchair
thin, pale, short gray hair
eyes dull and distant
clutching a worn dolly
lost inside herself
waiting patiently
for the end

Death

Do I fear death?

Will I die like Mom,
Alone from an aneurism
At night on the floor
By the side of the bed
Or like Nettie,
Unexpectedly while sleeping
Or Beau, on a hunting trip?

Will I endure great suffering
From some painful form of cancer
Or like Dad,
Slowly from complications of dementia?
Will I see death approaching
Like a tornado, or
Will it sneak up on me like a predator?

Will I accept death willingly,
Or fight it with passion?
Is it death I fear,
Or not knowing how it will end?

Defining Moments

When cancer returns
Another round of chemo,
Or let nature run its course.

When disaster strikes
Rebuild in the same place,
Or move to a new location.

When death takes a loved one
Decide never to hurt again,
Or choose to love again.

When a mother miscarries
Try again to become pregnant,
Or choose to adopt a child.

When you don't succeed
Throw in the towel,
Or pick up and try again.

Sometimes fate changes our plans,
But often it's our choices,
In those defining moments
That change our lives forever.

Entering The ER

People entering the ER
Tenseness furrowed foreheads
In waves of worry
Eyes strained with concern
Baring the anticipation
Of dreaded possibilities
Shoulders pressed down
By weighted fear of the unknown
Enveloped in mental and physical despair

People entering the ER
Holding loved ones hands
Triggered by a sense of possible loss
A dam of hope holding back a flood of tears
A tsunami of heartache ready to be unleashed
Trembling hands, the human Richter scale
Indicative of the body's quake within
Desperately trying to suppress
The volcanic eruption of emotions

Everyday Heroes

Mothers and fathers
Everyday heroes
Struggling to create a home, a family
Sacrificing their own needs, wants and desires
Working to provide the necessities of life
Food, clothing, and shelter
Creating a sanctuary of love, kindness and caring
A garrison for moral support,
Watching a family grow out of love,
Whose reward might be a kiss or hug.

Fourth Grade

Around fifth grade,
Dad built a house
with the GI Bill
moved out to the edge of the city
of Niagara Falls, last street
next to farmland where I learned to love the outdoors
I ran through tall corn fields with new friends
picked and ate green pears before they ripened
from an old abandoned orchard,
picked wild concord grapes and
collected hickory nuts and glossy chestnuts
swished through crispy maples leaves
that covered the sidewalks in autumn
hid in the loft of Melville's dairy barn
and built small forts and jumped into hay piles below
before being discovered and literally kicked out on our behinds
by the farmers oldest son
We tried to catch wild kittens in the barn, but never could
Biked out to another farm to see the newborn Holstein calves
and the horses stable where we picked our favorite
and pretended it was our own
We climbed oak and elm trees
picked wild strawberries and discovered their savory flavor
sweeter than store bought
Caught pollywogs and green frogs and toads, being careful not to get warts
Listened to the crickets and frogs croaking at night
and in the day, jets that thundered overhead from the nearby air force base
rattling mom's new kitchen cupboards
Smelled the fresh cut hay in the field behind the house
enjoyed the hollyhocks and iris in the farmer's wife's garden
in the middle of the unpaved country road before it was paved

Grandma's Fear

Was it my imagination,
Grandma's look of consternation?
Had she received misinformation
or had she missed a celebration?
Was it miscommunication
or did she fear an altercation?

No,
Grandma's look of consternation
was just her fear of constipation.

Happy Birthday Gina

It rained the day you were born,
yet my joy knew no bounds.
I was so happy I cried.
You were a fragile dream come true.
I wanted to shout to the world
that I had a daughter.
The first time I held you,
I believed in the miracle of life.
Each day you grew cuter and more lovable
and through your eyes
I began to see the world in a new way.

There were so many 'firsts',
your first word, your first tooth, your first steps,
You always greeted me at the door,
and I loved your hugs and kisses.
I loved to dance and sing with you.
I enjoyed sharing the wonders of nature with you.

As time passed I saw you change and grow.
Sometimes it hurt when you spread your wings,
and letting go wasn't easy.
Twenty-one years have passed since that day.
Now you're a beautiful young woman,
and I wouldn't have it any other way.

Funny it should rain on your birthday today,
but the joy and love I have for you,
is greater than I ever could have imagined.

Happy twenty-first birthday Gina.
I'll always love you.

Humor

Entertain a sense of humor
Exercise the facial muscles
Radiate a smile

Laughter
Sedative for pain and sorrow
Makes harsh realities palatable

A laugh, a chuckle, a giggle
A temporary shield against hurt
Escape from the mundane

Soothing balm
Enables emotional wounds
To heal

Humor allows us
To laugh at ourselves
See more clearly

Helps us navigate
The dark waters of life
With more perspective

Humor
A funny crutch
Keeps us moving

I Believe

Rejection, like ocean waves at high tide
tears at my writing dreams.

Rejection, like icy winter winds
freezes my flow of creativity.

Rejection, like hot summer sun,
dries up my reservoir of energy.

Yet, I believe persistence, like stars
clings to my writing aspirations.
Persistence, like the dawn,
brightens my feelings of hope.
Persistence, like spring
bursts forth with renewed inspiration,
and hope, like spiraling spring water
continues to surface with clarity.

Impressions

Impressions
Like electrical etchings,
Follow the path to my memory
To be caught in the web of my creativity,
Turning elusive thoughts
Into butterfly words
Which flutter on to the page before me.

Letting Go

the first time you leave your baby with a babysitter
the day you encourage your child to take their first steps without holding your hand
the first time you let your child ride away on a bicycle, or the day you drop them off
for their first day of daycare or school
the first time your child leaves for summer camp or goes out on a date
the day your child gets their driver's license and takes your car for a drive
the day you drop your child off for their first semester of college
the day your child gets married
the day you admit your parent into the nursing home
the day you cast a handful of dirt on the casket of a loved one
the day your dog or cat dies
the day you sell the home where you raised your family

Most of the time, we must let go in order to move on, but we always
seem to hold on to the time we let go, in our hearts forever.

Like Droplets of Water

When mountain snow melts
water droplets begin to trickle
and trickles form a stream.
It doesn't know which side
of the Continental Divide
the current will take it
as it winds and cascades.
Gravity and slope
determine the direction
east or west.

We are like droplets of water
not knowing where life will take us,
A journey of happiness
filled with love,
a journey of sadness
filled with heartache.
All we can do is live each day.
Try our best to make good choices,
accept the challenges presented
and make our journey count.

Little Children

Little children are like angels.
They fill our hearts with love and joy.
They're the future of tomorrow,
precious girls and precious boys.

Little children are like angels.
They give us laughter, bring us cheer,
give a reason to be living,
so let us hold them near.

When we need someone to love us,
when the world is not so grand,
they give us hugs and kisses,
snuggle close and hold our hand.

Little Things

A baby grasps your finger with a tiny hand, or
a toddler holds yours to walk.

A loved one's hug makes you know they care, and
a handshake lets you know everything's all right.

A young child picks a precious dandelion for you, and
a grandmother bakes your favorite apple pie.

A brilliant tangerine sunrise flares up the sky over a dark snowy landscape.
A morning meadowlark greets you with a long awaited song after winter.

The scent of lilacs permeates the air with its purple perfume.
A hot cup of coffee or tea warms your hands.

You savor a juicy peach freshly picked, or
fresh raspberry jam made from summer's bounty sweetens your tongue.

The night shimmers with nature's glitter of scattered stars.
The color waves of Northern Lights paint over the black canvas night.

The quilt made especially for you envelopes you in comfort.
A glass of ice tea or lemonade refreshes you in the heat of summer.

The sizzling smell of breakfast bacon wafts from the kitchen, or
the delicious aroma of chocolate chip cookies fresh from the oven drifts in the air.

Love Letters

Remember when

Love letters were
Sealed and kissed
Sent from someone
You loved and missed.

Remember when

Love letters were
Scented with rose
Held in your hand
Sniffed with your nose.

Remember when

Love letters were
Cursive in style
Warmed your heart
Made you smile.

Remember

Memories

Like a favorite shirt fades
or joyful daffodils shrivel
to brown tissue,
so do memories over time.

Like old newspapers that yellow
with headlines now forgotten,
and unnamed photos not recalled,
so do memories over time.

Recollections become mixed,
thoughts confused and muddled
dates and names lost forever,
so do memories over time.

Like frost destroys tomato plants
and scented flowers destined to die
friends and family recognition escapes,
so do memories over time.

The Blessing of Wyoming

Wyoming residents
are grateful having been spared
much of the suffering.
We enjoyed fresh air outdoors,
free to roam vast grasslands,
massive mountains carved by nature,
furrowed deep canyons, and valleys
sewn together by icy streams.
We watched herds
of mountain reigning elk
and prairie pronghorn.

Each new day was a gift.
Even the drought and winds
couldn't dry out our spirit.

Board games, puzzles and books
became important again.
We looked after each other
neighbor helping neighbor
despite long distances.
We nourished our faith and
appreciated more family time.
We reached out to old friends
became even more aware of
the people and the natural
blessings of Wyoming.

On a Positive Note

On a positive note
Covid19 has made people
Aware of what's really important.

A majority of people have slowed down,
Spent more quality time with family members
Revived family interest in board games and puzzles
Allowed for time to read, write, paint or garden
Encouraged some to start new hobbies and crafts
Permitted us time to clean out closets and file cabinets
Given many a deeper appreciation for the outdoors

Covid19 has made people
Aware of what's really important.

Made people grateful for a job and food on the table
A realization of how much we need each other
Caused people to reach out to others in need
Rethink vocations and revisit their faith
Inspired creative problem solving
Reminded us to reconnect and call old friends
Made us aware not to take life for granted

Covid19 has made people
Aware of what's really important.

School Teacher

You entrust your children to me
five days a week,
about seven hours a day.

I accept them the way they are
and work to make them
the best they can be.

I support them in their efforts
to discover, explore and learn
and develop their gifts and talents.

I'm there to help teach them
the ropes, survival tactics
for the everyday world.

I watch them grow
mentally and physically,
guide them on their way.

I grow to love them
as if they were my own,
then I let them go.

I send them on their way,
to another teacher to carry on
the education of your children.

Secret to Longevity

I asked the 100 year old man,
tell us your secret if you can.
How have you managed to live for so long?
Was it beautiful women, stout beer or song?

Here's the secret for living a long life.
Find a good woman, make her your wife.
The rest is simple, you must always pass
don't hold back when you have gas.

Snippets of a Young Child's Memories

Measles, hot summer day
Covered in a heavy wool blanket
Bedroom window shades down
Wearing sunglasses
Mom at my bedside

Mrs. Lynch, neighbor next door
Small porch with flower boxes
Fragrant ruffled purple petunias
Glass of milk and fresh
Warm, baked cookies

My little red wagon
Playing pioneers
Old white sheet and tree branches
Trying to make a covered wagon
Frustrated and gave up

Bundled up in gray snowsuit
Frigid winter day
Mom checking clothesline
Large white sheets
Frozen stiff in the breeze

Dad's payday
Home from shopping
Sitting on the floor drawing
In front of the stove
New coloring book and crayons

Bed time in my room
Snuggled in a big double bed
Between lots of stuffed animals
Staring at the huge closet doors
Afraid of the Boogeyman

Grandma's city apartment
The third floor parlor
Alone, nobody watching
Grandpa in a casket
Touched his dead hand

Thank You, Lord

Thank you, Lord, for the mountains.
You made them strong to lighten our burdens,
where cathedral rock spires lead our eyes to heaven,
and wildflowers, colorful and sweet, sharpen our senses.

Birds soar and lift our thoughts to greater heights,
and streams sparkle with the music of life, refreshing our spirits.
Gentle breezes soothe and calm our souls,
and radiant sunshine warms our bodies.
Sturdy trees teach us to bend,
and silence enables us to hear our hearts.

Thank you, Lord, for the mountains, their beauty and their life,
and for friends and loved ones, to share in your creation,
enjoying and reflecting upon its natural treasures,
and then quietly turning them into loving memories.

The Cleaning Lady

Walked into the post office
Greeted by the cleaning lady
I nodded with a smile
Paused for a moment
She wished me a good morning
Stopped cleaning the floor
Leaned on her mop handle
Studied me for a moment

"How are you today?"
"Fine… and you?"
"Good. It's a beautiful day."
"You work hard to keep the entry
Looking clean and shiny."
She shrugged and smiled
"I enjoy working here."
Chatted a bit more

Learned she was a former
Mental health therapist
Licensed clinical social worker
Left the position, too much stress
Takes pride in her work
More relaxed, slower paced
Appears peaceful and content
Appreciative of each day

The Gambler

King of his own land
Queen always at his side
Jack of all trades
Puts all his money on the table
Yet often dealt a joker
A bad hand
Win or lose
Always, a farmer or rancher.

The Old Lady

She sits in her rocker
staring at the photos
surrounding her
lost in memories.

Her wedding photo
speaks of faded beauty
and love passed away.

Gone, the uniformed son
who gave his young life
serving his country.

The children now grown
once nursed and diapered
cared for and loved.

Grandchildren who gave her
a second chance to see
through the eyes of a child.

The door bell rings
startles her back from the past
as she wipes away a tear.

She clutches her crocheted purse
opens the door where her ride waits
to take her to Sunday service
where hope still lives in her heart.

Twenty–One

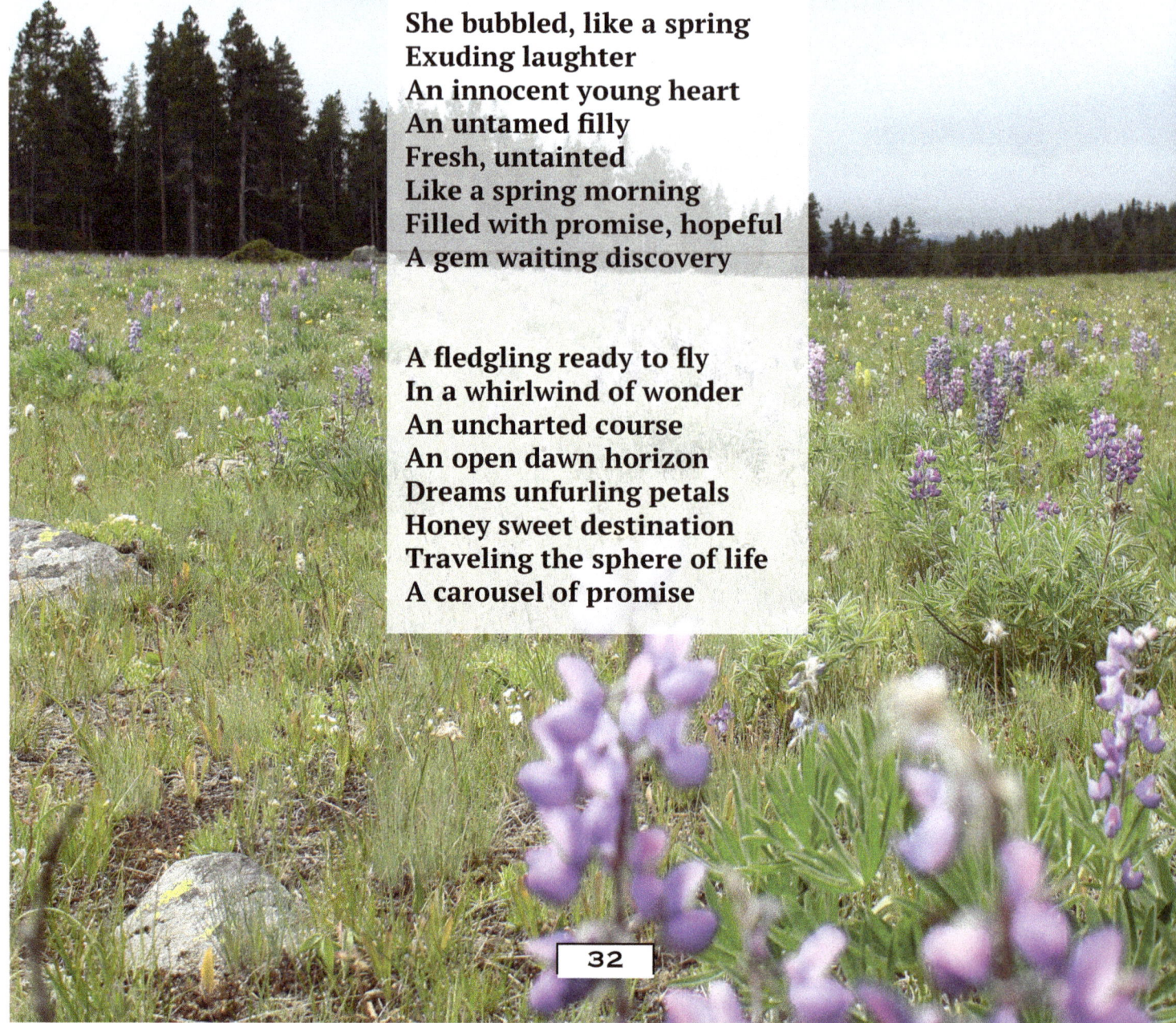

She bubbled, like a spring
Exuding laughter
An innocent young heart
An untamed filly
Fresh, untainted
Like a spring morning
Filled with promise, hopeful
A gem waiting discovery

A fledgling ready to fly
In a whirlwind of wonder
An uncharted course
An open dawn horizon
Dreams unfurling petals
Honey sweet destination
Traveling the sphere of life
A carousel of promise

Weary Traveler

Walking along highway 16, near Caribou Lodge, alone at dusk,
I watch the forest fade into the mountains,
and the mountains disappear into the darkness.
An awesome serenity takes hold of me.
The end of my day has finally dawned.
Yet the oncoming headlights remind me that others are still traveling,
and this timeless moment is only a pleasant pause in my life.
The highway goes on into nature's night and the lodge lights beckon,
so I must continue on…

Wounds

Physical wounds heal
Cuts and scratches scab over
Surgical incisions
Stitched or stapled closed
All leave visible scars

Emotional wounds
Not visible
May be covered
Festering over time
Poisoning a person

Personal wounds
Spread like bacteria
Infecting the human spirit
Polluting and distorting the mind
Fogging the clarity of reality

Young Man

Young man,
Beard and tattooed
Hospital housekeeping
Wondered
What's his story?
What's behind the mask and hazel eyes?
Struck up a conversation
Discovered more than his youth suggested
Or his badge stated

Lived in Spain and Turkey
Twenty four-year-old marine
Served in Afghanistan
Worked with the CIA
Knew the burden
Of carrying a gun
Fought for our country
Suffered knee, back and brain injuries
Still haunted by PTSD

Seventeen-year-old brother
Shot and killed
While trying to help a friend
War's separation cost him his marriage
Musical, writes and sings his own songs
Like *Freedom Ain't Fair*
Strums his guitar to the depths of his soul
Has goals - pay off mortgage …
Dreams - start a business…
Start a new life with hope
Built on the scars of the past

Glad I spoke to him
I would have missed
This unseen patriot

Annie

I sit in the rocker
Listening to the fountain
Bubbling about nothing.
The aspen leaves tremble
In fear of autumn.
The melon colored day lilies
Salute the setting sun
While black-eyed Susan
In gold petal attire
Shamelessly flaunt their beauty.

It's tranquil
But my heart is heavy.
Our 12-year-old dog
Annie, is gone.
No shining brown eyes,
Set in gold fluffy fur
Looking back at me.

No longer there
To greet me at the door.
I'll walk alone now.
The last of shedding hair
Has been vacuumed away.
The dog bed set aside.
Her leash lies empty.
Stainless steel bowls stored.

The red of ripening apples
Cannot cheer me today.
Late summer is
A time to bury dreams
And a canine companion.

Bluebirds

The bluebirds return every spring,
and oh the joy that they bring.
In a box by the window they nest,
to raise their young without rest.

The birds have made it quite clear;
They don't mind me being near.
I smile as I watch them fly by,
these creatures the color of sky.

During winter's darkness I yearn,
for my feathered friends to return.
Spring's special gift for me,
nature, always wild and free.

Bull's Eye

Alone in a prairie pasture
Parched grasses and sagebrush
A solid statue of muscle and might
Stands an Angus bull
Night black hide
Eyes of obsidian and elegant eyelashes
Stares over the landscape

What is he thinking?
Does he long for companionship?
Water to cool is arid tongue?
Is he aware of his fate?
Does he care?

Does he recall cooler, happier days,
When he frolicked with other calves?
Does he remember the mother that nursed him?
The man that tagged his ear
And burned his brand on him?

What lies behind those glistening eyes?

Max

Obsidian black coat
Eyes filled with mischief and love
Frolicking, curious, playful
My Black Lab pup grew
Into my friend, my companion,
Traveling and hunting buddy,
Always there for me,
By my side, listening, comforting.
Always happy to see me,
Ready to greet me
With wagging rubber hose tail
And bologna pink tongue,
With a nose like no other.
A free spirit, stubborn, strong willed
Always hungry, a garbage hound
Doing the "Poop Dance"
With stinky ears and missing toe,
Target of porcupine, skunk and thunder
Huffy Puppy, Moose's Patoot, or Old Man
Maxwell, Max, my dog, my best friend.

Bridges

A bridge connects
One side to the other
Steel or wooden, short or long
Wide or narrow, doesn't matter
It's a strong connection
Whether it crosses a creek or river
A ravine or majestic canyon,
A railroad or a highway

A bridge separates
It separates love and hatred
Lies and truth,
Fantasy from reality
Anger and forgiveness
Strength and weakness
Good from evil, right from wrong
Selfishness and compromise

We encounter bridges everyday
In one way or another
Bridges between life and death
Childhood and maturity
Bridges aren't easy and take time
Perhaps the most difficult bridge
Will be between faith and doubt
Between this world and the next

Contrast

The hospital entrance
A large atrium
Natural light
Towering Christmas tree
Brightly twinkling
A festive entry way

Silver icicles grace boughs
Gold ribbons fall in swirls
White snowflakes brighten
Red poinsettias deck the planters

The emergency entrance
Next to the atrium
Artificially lit low ceiling
Sterile, serious business
A giant potted peace lily
Among the metal armed chairs

Silver steel instruments
Gold ring on injured finger
White bandage wrapped on wound
Red blood stained shirt

Dreams in the Wind

I pass them while driving on the interstate
Or Wyoming roads and highways
A few Chinese elms or pines
Maybe a lilac bush or two.
They give a sense of having been planted
To provide shade or protection
From the pressing winds.

The houses are gone,
Like the settlers who once lived there
With their dreams blown away with the wind.
Gusts pass through the abandoned tree survivors
Carrying dust, dead leaves and bits of debris
Unimportant like the lives now gone.

Do the dreams of people who pass
Still linger in the wind
Perhaps filtering into the minds
Of those people living downwind?

Flight

I'm at the mercy of technology
and the control of unfamiliar people
My life is in their hands as
I settle into trusted flight

Encapsulated in a steel vessel
earth becomes a 3-D topographical map
Land becomes contorted with ruffled ribbon ridges
and serpent bands of rivers and streams
Dimpled foothills give way to stoic peaks
of the Rocky Mountains cloaked
in robes of late autumn snow

Cities, towns and villages
resemble electronic keyboards
Ponds, lakes and reservoirs a
myriad of shapes and sizes mirror
the mood of the sky
Highways mere threads of concrete
beside square and circular fields
of corn and wheat create
intricate visual quilts

Sunlight filters through clouds like shredded shards
of pink insulation. The clouds
become a shrouded mist enveloping
blue sky and then transforming into
a white nothingness, vast yet contained.
I'm thrust into the future - a life I cannot see.

I-25 Cheyenne to Chugwater

Lost in the tired landscape of November

my eyes follow the barbed wire fences
which hold the land together.

Waves of wheat and cinnamon colored grasses,
blend with dried and withered wildflowers.

Pine and juniper wind breaks
arch along ridges in graceful lines.

Shaved almond grasses edge the interstate
with pockets of green quilled yucca.

Windmills silhouette the sky
like delicate charcoal etchings.

Old cottonwoods and Chinese elm
barricade ranch homesteads.

Red dogwood and yellow stemmed willow
worm their way up winding creek beds.

On the horizon pale blue peaks
of the Laramie range beckon me.

Nearing the nestled town of Chugwater
a metal cowboy and dog overlook the prairie.

A bold billboard proudly shouts
Home of Chugwater Chili.

The long stretch of interstate in November
has its own special beauty.

The Funeral Home

Chilled to help preservation
Warmed by hugs of loved ones
Firm handshakes ensure support
Sad smiles meant to cheer
Subtle soft whispers of respect

Sudden burst of uncontrolled laughter,
That lighten the veil of death's heavy mantle

The fragrance and beauty of flowers
Help sweeten death's bitter taste
Photos of loved ones to help us
Remember the good times
Solemn place to celebrate a loss of life

Autumn's Smokey Landscape

As I look out my office window
To the eastern sunrise
The smoky haze continues to
Smother the landscape.

The dawning sun struggles
To lift itself from the horizon
A rose colored ball subdued by
Feathered clouds.

Under the sheath of darkness
Autumn tiptoed over
The narrow leafed cottonwoods
Revealing their undercoats of gold.

Uncertainty looms as
Flocks of blackbirds
Wisk through the air
Aware of fleeting summer.

Sadness looms over my sullen heart
Like a black veil descending
Suffocating the last breath of summer
Abandoning hope and lost dreams.

Calendar of Trees

Trees
Greeters of spring
Season of promise
Bedecked in green
Adorned in blossoms
Paper white petals
Perfect pink and rose blush

Trees
Breath of summer
Season of life
Dressed in emerald garb
Grasping endless sky
Shading, waving, fluttering
Inviting feathered friends

Trees
Artist of autumn
Season of bounty
Fruit and nut laden
Splashed apple and rusty red
Burnished gold and brilliant yellow
A flamboyant farewell

Trees
Guardians of winter
Season of rest
Evergreens clad in wedding white
Transparent deciduous
Branches woven into the sky
Keyboard for wind songs

Winter

Winter
the cold, seemingly heartless
season of death
is the seedbed for spring
the groundwork for regeneration
foundation for new life
table for a different setting.

Winter
A time for meditation
An evaluation of life
Reassessing goals
Preparation for the future
Planning, dreaming
A rejuvenation of sorts.

Winter
an invitation to appreciate
what is to come.

Avalanche

Avalanche
A tsunami of snow
An explosive wave
Of destructive energy
Hurdled down a precarious slope
Thundered to the tranquil valley below

Eliminated all obstacles
Entangled two friends
Unsuspecting skiers
In its ruthless rampage
One lived, one died
changed the lives of many

Valentine's Day 2021
Marred by death

Campfire

Coals burn memories into the heart
As swirling smoke rises like incense
With each campers' inner thoughts
Up in to the blanket of night.
Stars, once sparks for heartfelt dreams
Glitter like shattered windshield glass.

Campfire, a circle of light and warmth
Provides a sense of restful security
In the tranquil mountain forest.
Generations of family and friends
Sharing laughter and life's stories
Bonding over toasted marshmallows.

Dandelion

Sometimes I wish
I was a dandelion
A bright reflection
Of the solar star
Lazily floating among warm
Dark green blades of grass
Brightening the day
A cheery delight for a child
To gift their mother

Then to become a tuft
Of paratrooper seeds
White angels to take flight
When a child makes a wish
Then blows me windward
Into a blazing blue sky
Where I can land anywhere
And begin my life again

Darkness

Without darkness
Would we appreciate light?

A candle's glow
A campfire's warmth
The radiance of starlight
The comfort of moonlight

The brilliance of sunrise
The safety of street lamps
Airport runway lights
A lighthouse beacon

Without darkness
Would we appreciate light?

Each Seed

Every seed
Has the ability
To germinate and grow
But many never reach
Their full potential
Killed by the cold
Dried up by the sun
Drowned by the rain

The very things that
Nourish life
Often destroy it

Long Journeys

My heart takes my mind on long journeys
Past the day's routine to higher thoughts
Woven into a timeless tapestry
Of morning mountains and eloquent simplicity.

It drifts with the seasons, lost and lonely
Caring only for the sanctity of sheltered forests
Where joy splashes on tumbled granite
And peace waits in sunny solitude.

Reborn to the tranquil tide of clouds
And the petals passing of beauty, my mind
Wanders, and wonders why it must ever return.
My heart takes my mind on long journeys.

November Cottonwoods

Narrow leaved cottonwoods
Meshed together along the creek
Trunks rise from wheat colored
Blankets of dried withered grass

Scattered among the sagebrush
Glacial granite boulders
Nature's tombstones
Strewn among the landscape

Arched, crooked, stretching, reaching
Curled, twisted, tangled and gnarled
A myriad of limbs and intricate branches
Intertwined cottonwoods silhouette the sky

Phantom Clouds

Tufted waves of cotton
ruffled pink and gold,
fade into the darkness;
the cloak of night unfolds.

Pallor hues of sunset
tint the evening sky,
form the coral phantoms
which animate the sky.

Distant waves of color
stream endlessly above;
drift into the heavens
of pastel which I love.

Silver Lake

There is a lake so far away,
where once I spent a peaceful day.

Where flowers bloom in sheer delight
and n'er a sound is heard at night,
except for night birds on the wing
and in the morning bluebirds sing.

While chipmunk chatter echoes through
the sweet and misty forest dew,
and running swiftly as a stream
are graceful deer with eyes that gleam.

The pristine lake is cool and clear
a placid silver plated mirror.
Its diamond beauty unsurpassed
reflects the cotton clouded mass.

And when at last the day is done
and darkened night has almost come,
the sun becomes a gold doubloon,
soon replaced by mirrored moon.

There is a lake so far away,
where once I spent a peaceful day.

Snowflakes

Snowflakes

White

Graceful

Swirling, twirling

Dancing downward ballerinas

Snowflakes

Fluffy

Cottony

Frosted flowers

Drifting downy feathers

The Birth of Day

The heavens bleed
Across the winter sky
A volcanic glow
A dark layer
Of cloud cover
Dampens it
Extinguishing
The flames of dawn
Inviting another cold
December day

Soon a pale purplish red
Sliver of sky
Severs the horizon
Burns the background
For the somber silhouettes
Of winter weary trees
Black skeletons of the season

Frigid winds lift the mantle
Exposing another fiery glow
Finally the sun fractures the clouds
Into fragments of a blazing
Winter morning
Tempered with a watercolor brush
Of bluish tones and
Splinters the sky

Morning has freed herself from night
Giving birth to day

The Garden Cherub

A lone cherub statuette
nestled among a carpet
of sedum and juniper
adorns the edge of
the frosted flower garden
in anticipation of spring.

Surrounded by mounds
of silken snow
nature's winter mantle
a serene reminder of
peace and beauty
awaiting us in death.

The Log

A towering
centennial cottonwood
now hugs the ground.

A larva laden log
returns to earth
a thriving community
of bustling ants and beetles.

A silent unseen center of activity
busily changing the landscape
preparing the site for
the next generation,
creating new life from death.

Unnoticed

Every flower in the field
wants to be noticed
for the beauty it has to offer.

Yet only a few, if any
will be recognized
and appreciated.

Water's Power

Water, nature's essence of life
Gentle like spring rains or mist
Strong like rapids and waterfalls

Fluid, trickles, sprays, spatters
Gurgles, rushes, plunges and carves
Creates rainbows and reflections

Water has a music all its own
Rhythmic splashing waves and bubbling streams
Roaring surf, flashfloods and tsunamis

Water is a raindrop, stream, creek, river,
Puddle, pond, lake, sea, ocean
Water sustains life and destroys it

Water, one of nature's greatest powers

White Asters

Dry prairie grasses edge the county road
White asters mingle among the clusters
Of yellow sticky gum weed
And mounds of Broom Snakeweed.
Fields of irrigated green contrast
Against distant rolling umber hills,
Etched with red rock scoria.
Hoards of grasshoppers
Pop aimlessly within the landscape.
Days shorten at season's end.

Wrath of the Wind

While listening to every sound
I lay there quiet and still.
The lightning seared at the land
and thunder tossed in the hills.

Wild was the wrath of the wind
that breathed on the cabin door.
She moaned like a dying soul,
at the weathered roof she tore.

Her restless fury frightening
as the waves teased at the shore.
Like the damnation of earth,
she seethed outside my door.

Her anger grew much stronger,
whirlwinds danced on the sea.
She tore through the cabin door
and she waltzed away with me.

Wyoming Watershed

a myriad of lodge pole pine
blanket the mountains
intermingled with fluttering aspen
mountain maple and chokecherry

pine trees cling
to granite cliff sides
with gnarled finger roots
wrapped around boulders

at the lower elevations
ponderosa pine stand proud
their reddish brown trunks
bold in the sun

pine needles matt into
soft spoken paths
spring green moss
dress rocks and trees

meadows of lupine and
gold balsam root
blend into quilts
sewn together by glistening streams

grassy parks beckon elk and deer
beneath them a web of root systems
woven into the fabric of earth
tightly holding the soil

summer snow fields
fir and alpine wildflowers
rock, wind and rain
nature's watershed

April Snow

If you live in the Rockies, you must know
That April brings the chance of snow.
While earth awakens from her sleep,
Snow may pile up fast and deep.
But soon this too shall melt away
And bring the verdant green of May.

Wyoming's Pallet of Color

Ultramarine of sky and blue drifts of lupine
Blood red of Indian paintbrush and scarlet gillia
Burnt orange of sunsets and rocky buttes
Spring green of meadows and carpet moss

Brilliant yellow blossoms of balsam root and meadowlarks
Pastel purple of twilight and flowers of the shooting star
Perfection pink of wild geranium and roses
Forest green of conifer blankets of pine, spruce and fir

Pristine white of mountain snow and gleaming glaciers
Stone gray of granite peaks and chattering squirrels
Burnt sienna of deer and elk and ponderosa bark
Glossy black of obsidian rock and satin black of night sky

Author Biography:

Known by many as the teacher who dances on his desk, Eugene M. Gagliano (pronounced Galiano) is a retired elementary teacher whose author presentations are entertaining, informative and inspirational. He has presented at 182 schools, and at IRA, teacher, SCBWI, and library conferences, and for libraries and festivals in Wyoming, Colorado, Missouri, South Dakota, Minnesota, Montana, Nebraska, Texas and Hawaii. Gene was the recipient of the IRA's 2004 Wyoming State Celebrate Literacy Award and the 2001 Arch Coal Teacher Achievement Award. Gene's book Dee and the Mammoth illustrated by Zachary Pullen, won the 2010-2011 Wyoming State Historical Society Award for Best Fiction. *Dee and the Mammoth represented the state of Wyoming at the National Book Festival in Washington, D.C in 2011. His other books include C is for Cowboy, a Wyoming Alphabet; Four Wheels West, a Wyoming number Book (a former Western Writer's Spur Award nominee); V is for Venus Flytrap, a Plant Alphabet; My Teacher Dances on the Desk (winner of the 2010 Delaware Diamonds Book List Children's Choice Award); Secret of the Black Widow (a former Wyoming Indian Paintbrush Award nominee); The Magic Box; Falling Stars; Inside the Clown; Booger; Little Wyoming; Angel's Landing; Is It True? (2017 children's humorous poetry book); Snap(2019) 2nd place 2019 Evvy Award winner and Wedge of Fear(2018) 3nd place 2019 Evvy Award winner. In 2021, his poetry collection, a 122 page hard cover and colorfully illustrated book, A Wyoming State of Mind was released. He is a graduate of the Institute of Children's Literature, is a member of Western Writers, Society of Children's Book Writers and Illustrators, Wyoming Writers, Wyoming Poets, Johnson County Arts & Humanities Council, Friends of the Library, and is on the Wyoming Arts Council Artists Roster. Gene is the Wyoming State Poet Laureate. His book Is It True ? was selected as the state of Wyoming's Best Read for 2018 for the National Book Festival in Washington, DC. Gene's latest children's poetry book What Did You Say? (2021) is the sequel to Is It True? Check out his website at www.gargene.com or his face book author page at www.facebook.com/dancingteacher.

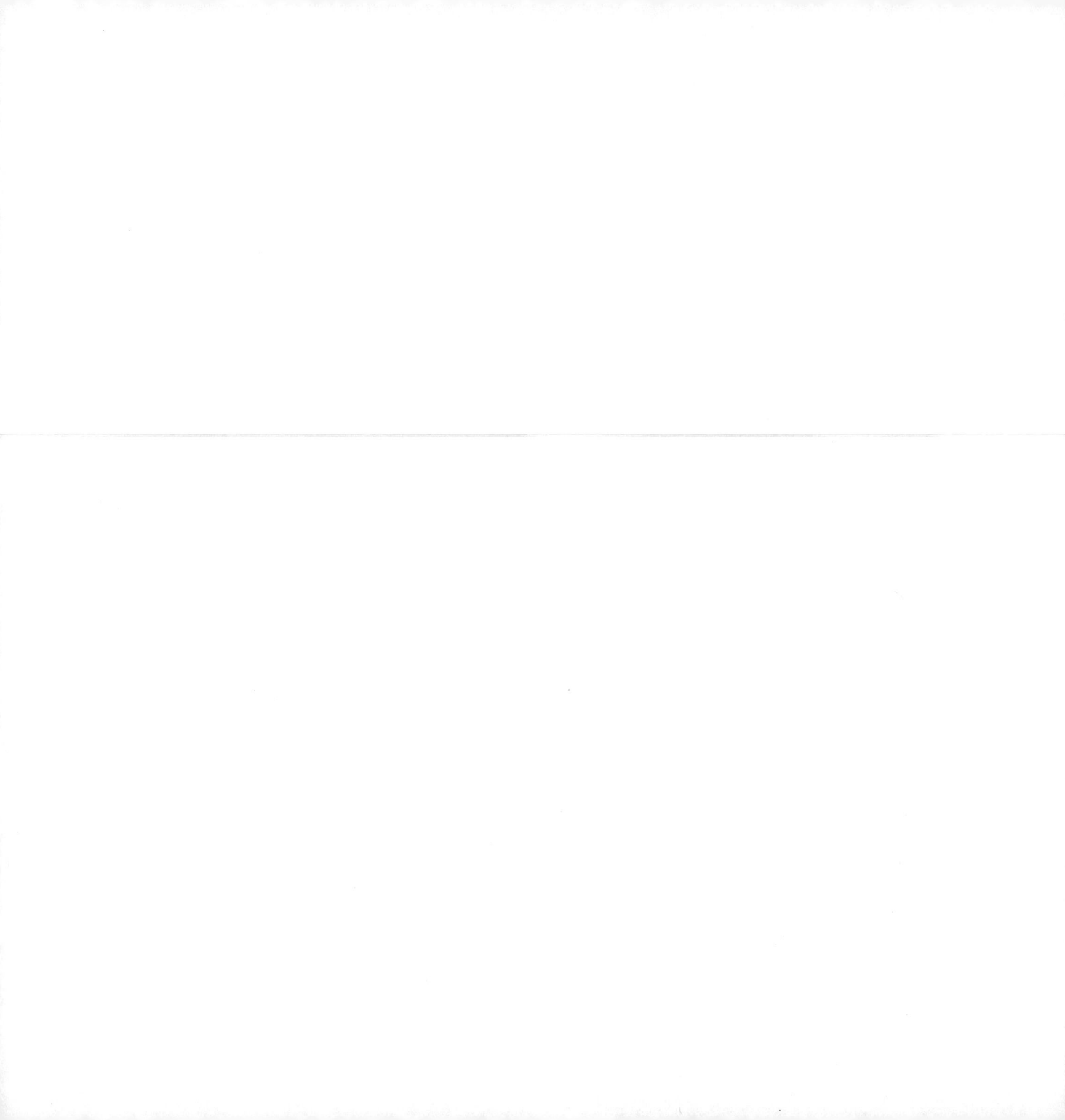

www.ingramcontent.com/pod-product-compliance
Lightning Source LLC
Chambersburg PA
CBHW061120170426
43209CB00013B/1615